BN5/02

BN5/02

# RUSSIAN ALBUM

*Florence Farmborough at a forest dressing station*

# RUSSIAN ALBUM
## 1908-1918

## FLORENCE FARMBOROUGH

*Edited by*
JOHN JOLLIFFE

## MICHAEL RUSSELL

First published in Great Britain 1979
by Michael Russell (Publishing) Ltd.,
The Chantry, Wilton, Salisbury, Wiltshire

Typeset in Monotype Imprint
by Mouldtype Foundry Ltd., Preston and London

Printed and bound in Great Britain
by Butler & Tanner Ltd., Frome, Somerset

ISBN 0 85955 039 7

# CONTENTS

# INTRODUCTION

Florence Farmborough was born in 1887 at Steeple Claydon in Buckinghamshire. She had been named after Florence Nightingale, and while very young, she and her sister were taken for a walk past Claydon House, the seat of the Verney family, where the famous old lady was then staying as the guest of Sir Edmund Verney (a stepson of Florence Nightingale's sister, Parthenope,) and his wife, Lady Margaret. When the children passed the house, Florence Nightingale appeared at an upstairs window, as had been promised, and waved to them.

In 1908, Florence Farmborough went to Russia to teach English to some Russian children, first in Kiev and, later, in Moscow, where she became 'one of the family' of a leading heart specialist, Dr. Pavel Sergeyevitch Ousov. When the war broke out, in 1914, she trained as a VAD in the military hospital organised by Princess Golitsin. After six months, she successfully passed several examinations in Russian and qualified as a surgical hospital nurse. She then enrolled in the 10th Red Cross Surgical Field *Otryad* of the *Zemski Soyuz* and except for, leave spent in Moscow and a month in the Crimea, recuperating from a serious illness, she remained on active service until the *Otryad* was forced by the Bolsheviks to disband in the late autumn of 1917.

She had fortunately already begun to keep a photographic record of her stay in Russia. After the outbreak of war, she began also to keep a diary. When it was published in an edited form in 1974, together with some of the photographs from her collection, she received more than 800 letters from all over the world, many of them from complete strangers. As well as the endless praise that greeted the text, one reviewer wrote 'The photographs are exceptionally interesting, and we hope some day that they will be collected together as a picture book.' Her *Russian Album 1908–1918* fulfils that hope. Pictorial records of the war on the Eastern Front are comparatively rare, and when one remembers the circumstances of chaos and collapse, it is hardly surprising how little has survived. The pictures, therefore, apart from their human impact, have an unusual importance as a historical record. In this field Pasternak's masterpiece is familiar to millions. Here is the world of Doctor Zhivago seen through the eyes of a heroic Englishwoman.

Tending the wounded, and doing whatever was possible to ease the suffering of the dying, this was to be her daily task, often for extended periods, and with a complete absence of regular hours (or quarters) for either sleep or meals. Now and again there would be a lull. Military units would go into reserve, together with the Red Cross staff attached to them, and others would take their places. Through the long Russian winters, the fighting was brought to a standstill by ice and snow; but then, as always, there was the host of homeless refugees, starving and freezing, whose claims on the Red Cross were just as urgent and impossible to refuse as those of the military. But there were also, from time to time, opportunities to use the camera – on colleagues, patients, soldiers, the landscape, and the ravages of the battlefield. Nothing could express more vividly the nature of being at war, with its horrors, its contrasts, and its paradoxes, than the story Miss Farmborough tells through these photographs. However exhausting, the work was also fulfilling, and it had the effect of making her, so to speak, fall in love with the idea of relieving the suffering of friend and enemy alike – Germans, Austrians and Turks, as well as Russians, Cossacks and Ukrainians, and Khirgiz troops from Turkestan.

Then, in March 1917, the Tsar abdicated. Kerensky, Minister of War in the new Provisional Government, introduced many reforms, bewildering to officers and men alike. Miss Farmborough heard him address the troops in the course of one of his tours of the Front. 'They recognised in him,' she has recalled, 'not only a great patriot but a very great and able leader.' His reforms, nevertheless, were followed by the disintegration and desertion of the Russian armies. The courage and endurance of the soldiers, the unshrinking work of the Red Cross, all now seemed to have been in vain. But, for the authoress of this book, what nobler and more worthwhile course could there have been to follow through those years? It is a story which makes nonsense of all purely materialistic theories of human life and actions, and it is a celebration of everything that is generous on the most heroic scale.

JOHN JOLLIFFE

The Russian Front Lines in
January 1915 and July 1917

———————— January 1915
– – – – – – – – July 1917

0   20        100
|___|__|__|__|__| miles

BALTIC

SEA

• Riga

EAST
PRUSSIA

Molodechno
• Grodno          Rakov
  Skidel        • Minsk
• Belostok      Neman

POLAND          Bobrysk •
                              • Zhlobin
• Warsaw                        Bryansk •
            Bug
        • Brest Litovsk   Kalinkovichi
  RUSSIA      •
        Vlodava    Mozyr •        Khutor Mikhaylovsk •
Vistula • Lyublin
      Holm              • Ovruch
                        • Koresten           • Konotop
Rzheshchuv •          • Novograd Volynskiy
  • Yaroslav        • Shepetovka    • Kiyev
Lemberg/Lvov •   Tarnopol
E. GALICIA     Podgaytsy • Volochisk • Starokonstantinov
             Skalat •
           Buchach •    • Kazatin
  Stanislav/ • Kopchintse  Vinnitsa
  Ivano-Frankovsk Chortkov •    • Zhmerinka
CARPATHIANS              UKRAINE
AUSTRIA—    • Chernovits   Dnestr
            Seret
HUNGARY   • Dorogoy
        Suchava • • Botushany        Dnepr
          Pashchany
            Yassy  Prut  Kishinev •
                                  Odessa •   Dnepr
                                            CRIMEA
ROUMANIA                              Simferopol •

Map devised by Kate Grimond, drawn by Patrick Leeson

# RUSSIA AT PEACE
## 1908-1914

I went to Russia in 1908. I was twenty-one, with an urge to travel that had been with me since my earliest years. Reflecting now upon my travels, I have said that I loved Russia the most because she taught me the meaning of the word 'suffering'. It was a lesson, of course, learned principally in the days of war and revolution; the Russia of my first acquaintance, glimpsed through these initial pages, will seem by contrast tranquil and remote.

I stayed first in Kiev. The photograph below shows two students of the university passing an old Jewish pedestrian in their light, backless *izvoshchik*. Kiev, ancient capital of the Ukraine and described in the chronicles as 'Mother' of Russian cities, had been a flourishing commercial centre well over a century before Moscow existed. The first sovereign Ukrainian state was established in the ninth century, but after long periods of harassment by hostile neighbours, this area of 'Little Russia' finally lost its sovereignty in the seventeenth century.

Kiev, too, had been the birthplace of Christianity in Russia. Prince Vladimir was baptised there in 988 and initiated the conversion of the Russian people. The event was commemorated there each year by the religious ceremony of 'Blessing the Waters'. I watched it in January 1909.

Architecturally, Kiev is a city of exceptional interest. Above is the imposing Cathedral of St. Vladimir, patron saint of Christian Russia. Its style would be described by architectural historians as 'pseudo-Byzantine' – perhaps rather ungenerous to a man who recruited the Greek clergy to evangelise his country and who married the sister of a Byzantine emperor! Like the more famous, and much earlier, Cathedral of St. Sophia in Kiev, St. Vladimir has an interior studded with icons, paintings, frescoes and mosaics.

Near Kiev is the beautiful and historic Pecherskaya Lavra, or Monastery of the Caves (now a museum). Founded in the eleventh century, it was visited annually by thousands of pilgrims. In the Catacombs of St. Anthony lay the embalmed bodies of many saints. Some of the caves, with their rows of coffins, penetrated under the River Dnieper, and were so narrow that pilgrims could only pass, candle in hand, single file. The monastery included a theological academy, in front of which the lower group is posed.

In the Orthodox Church calendar every *prazdnik*, or holiday, had its own ritual celebration, often centuries old. The magnificent icon on the right, above, consisted of a painting of the Virgin andChild, encrusted with pearls and jewels. It was being carried in procession to a village church, escorted by priests and nuns, where it would feature in a special service.

11

The Volga, with its 2,300 miles, is the longest river in Europe and is navigable throughout most of its course. This woodman, floating his timber downstream, was singing one of the many traditional songs of the river.

The home-made fishing tackle in the photograph below is not as rudimentary as it looks, and the remarkable skill of the Volga fishermen was handed down from father to son. The river was so rich in fish (including both salmon and sturgeon) that a fisherman in those days could make an easy and even lucrative living.

The *troika* was sleigh in winter and carriage in the summer. The horse in the centre was permitted only a very rapid trot, while the flankers cantered with heads turned outwards. In winter, gliding swiftly over the frozen snow, the *troika* seemed hardly to touch the ground – the only sound the soft thud of the horses' hooves and the jingle of the silver bells attached like necklaces to each bridle. The arched yoke, which fastened the shafts to the collar of the central horse, was often distinctively painted.

The typical peasant's home was no more than a wooden hut, commonly known as an *eezba*, frequently built by the occupant himself. The picture on the right shows a thriving family of ten children brought up in two cramped rooms. When I suggested taking their photograph, the father and the children posed eagerly for me outside the hut. The mother, who showed more signs of what must have been a tremendous domestic strain, preferred to remain inside, watching us through the window.

In many of the towns of Byelo-Russia and the Ukraine, the Jewish community exerted strong influence in the market place. The men above were shopkeepers, though that day, their Sabbath, the till was silent and they foregathered after the ceremonies of the synagogue for a sociable discussion. They would be strictly Orthodox Hebrews, scrupulously careful in observing their religion and its laws.

Almost every 'government', or province, of Imperial Russia had its own style of national dress, and the colourfully embroidered costumes provided much of the visible charm of rural life. The woman on the right, above, from the Ryazan province in Central Russia, had created a charming costume of her own. The young girl gathering sticks among the slender silver birches was Ukrainian. The women of the Ukraine were always renowned for their fine needlework and love of colours. Even when working at their ordinary daily tasks, they would wear a garland of flowers, with ribbons dangling round their heads, and strings of bright beads round their necks.

The party settling down to their black bread and samovar were woodmen, who had been cutting and storing wood for a *dacha*. The *dacha*, or country villa, provided an escape from urban life, most appreciated in the sultry days of summer. It ranged from the humble to the palatial, but was always built of wood and set in the shade of trees.

In the outskirts of country towns in the Ukraine you would see peasants like those opposite, above, laden with earthenware pots and jars secured to wooden frames. These were the country milkmen, arriving with fresh milk, cheese, whey and eggs for the townsfolk.

The peasant women in this area were as capable as the men at working in field and forest. At harvest time they would spend long hours wielding a sickle, often – like the woman opposite, below – accompanied by children too small to be left at home.

In contrast to the more elegant sleighs, built for style and speed, the peasants' vehicles, as above, were stoutly constructed, to convey heavy loads from door to door, and earn a few vital roubles.

The group below are Ruthenians, or Red Russians, who formed the bulk of the rural population in parts of south-west Russia.

This reminder of summer nightfall on the Black Sea still brings back for me the special beauty of that southern tip of the Crimean peninsula. The vineyards in the photograph opposite, above, were around Massandra, where the fertile soil was cultivated down to the last square foot.

Southern Crimea was called the Riviera of Russia, and thousands of the more prosperous Russians from the north would flock to its mild climate and exquisite scenery. One of the most fashionable resorts was Yalta, below, built at the foot of precipitous rocks, with the Bear Mountain towering to 1,800 feet in the background. Yalta was known as the 'Mecca of the Upper Ten'.

The other photograph opposite, below, is of the Monastery of the Assumption, hewn out of the rock at Bakhchisarai in the Crimea, once part of the last independent Tartar Khanate in Russia. Moscow was not free of the Tartars till 1480, after domination lasting 240 years. As they retreated south and east, they left scattered communities in remote places round the Black Sea and the Caucasian ranges.

The Tartar villages of the Crimea retained their racial characteristics, and among themselves the Tartars never spoke Russian. Even the poorest village children, like those in the picture opposite, above, were dressed in accordance with Tartar style and taste. I noticed, too, little Tartar girls with henna stains on fingers and face. Even in childhood they were taught to use henna as a cosmetic. The men in the picture are itinerant pedlars, who found ready buyers in the hotels for their silks, rugs, pearl necklaces, and other oriental delights.

In the lower photograph opposite, two draught oxen wait for their Tartar driver to harness them to a primitive field implement. The large building is a caravanserai, or bed-and-breakfast inn.

I was also able to visit the Caucasus and was impressed by the unusual grace and beauty of the women. The Caucasian girl above wears a long silk coat over loose silk trousers, with a scarlet pill-box cap, embroidered with pearls. The young Circassian on the right, proudly showing off his national costume, was four years old. He wears the *tcherkeska*, or long woollen coat, with its rows of cartridge cases, and the *papakha*, or high astrakhan cap. He flourishes a tiny silver dagger, plucked from the sheath hanging at his girdle. No doubt his warlike instincts are nourished by the fermented mare's milk ('koumiss') which forms part of his daily diet. He seems set to maintain the fighting traditions of the Cossacks.

In 1910 I had moved to Moscow, to live with the family of a prominent heart specialist, Doctor Pavel Sergeyevich Ousov. I taught English to his two daughters, Asya, who was nineteen, and Nadya, who was sixteen.

The Kremlin's glittering array of golden domes, towers, cupolas and crosses dominates the whole city of Moscow. Here the Tsars were crowned; here, in great pomp, they resided, and from here they issued their autocratic decrees. No newcomer to the city could fail to be impressed by the Kremlin's treasures. The *Tsar Kolokol*, or King Bell, the largest in the world, was cast in 1735, and is said to weigh 200 tons. While still in the foundry, it suffered a fatal crack, and instead of swinging on high, it is held permanently, and in a sense symbolically, earthbound.

My most vivid memory of the Kremlin is of seeing Tsar Nicholas, the Tsarina, and their children make their way from the Great Palace to the Cathedral of the Assumption. It was in August 1914. They were going, I remember, to pray for the Imperial Army's success against the German and Austrian aggressors.

Another showpiece (opposite, above) is *Tsar Poushka*, King Cannon, which was cast in 1586, measures 17 feet long and weighs just over 38 tons. Like the great bell, it was too massive ever to he used. The large cannon-ball on the right weighs nearly 2 tons.

Ever since the twelfth century, when Moscow was only a poor handful of wooden huts, the river Moskva has guarded the southern approach to the city's heart. Below, from the south-west corner of the old city, is a glimpse of the buildings added over the centuries within the Kremlin walls.

We would leave Moscow in the early summer. The scene overleaf (at a friend's *dacha*) symbolises for me the contrast between those prewar years and the tragic days to follow. The group, drinking tea and eating cherries, could almost have been characters in one of Chekhov's plays.

This is Nadya, picking spring flowers in the woods around the Ousovs' *dacha*, and below, dressed in peasants' costumes, Asya, Nadya and I are helping with the harvest. Modern methods and machines were quite unknown on Russian farms at this time. As in Tolstoy's famous descriptions, the scythe and the sickle were the reaper's only implements. But despite the long, hot hours of toil, the harvest gave a satisfaction all of its own, and the harvesters would often break into traditional country ballads that were handed down from generation to generation. Indeed singing was an accepted part of the routine.

At the beginning of August 1914, Germany declared war on Russia. I had been back to England for a holiday earlier in the year, and now we were all staying at the *dacha*, where the crisis seemed comfortably remote. German and Austrian troops, we heard, were massed on Russia's western borders, from the Roumanian frontier to the Baltic Sea. The news grew worse. England, France, Belgium and Russia were at war with Germany. I think, in my youthful enthusiasm, I saw it all more as challenge than calamity. Certainly I had no comprehension of the change that was about to engulf Russia.

# RUSSIA AT WAR
## 1914-1915

We were all determined to help. Then, in Moscow, we were seeing the first wounded soldiers back from the Front – from Poland, East Prussia and Galicia. One of the first hospitals in the city was Princess Golitsin's. Dr. Ousov had been appointed a member of the medical staff, and persuaded the Princess to allow Asya, Nadya and myself to work there as Voluntary Aids. So I celebrated that Christmas with the convalescent soldiers you see above. The Tsar and the Tsarina gaze down from the wall.

After six months' training in Princess Golitsin's hospital I had passed the seven examinations in Russian that were required and, along with Asya and Nadya, I was now qualified to become a member of

the Russian Red Cross. To my great joy I was accepted in the First *Letuchka*, or Flying Column, of the 10th Surgical Unit of the All-Russian *Zemski* (Provincial) *Soyuz*. Asya and Nadya were to stay on in the hospital: Asya was too delicate for service at the front, Nadya was still too young.

Our two Flying Columns each had a staff of four surgical sisters, a housekeeping sister, two surgeons and several hospital brothers, about thirty orderlies, and an officer, with an assistant, in charge of the stores and feeding arrangements. For transport, each *Letuchka* had two dozen light two-wheeled carts with canvas hoods, with the same number of horses. We also had two motor-cars and several two-horse drays.

27

We were to be sisters of the First and Second *Letuchka* [photographed in 1916: F.F., standing, second from left]. I had my precious Red Cross certificate; I was impatient to be off. We heard that our unit would be stationed for a time on the Austrian Front in the Carpathians. My nurse's wardrobe was augmented with boots and breeches for riding, and I bought a thick sheepskin waistcoat for winter wear – its Russian name, *dushegreychka*, meant 'soul-warmer'. Then, finally, on Wednesday, 11th March, we were ready to go. Anna Ivanova Ousov, my Russian 'mother', gave me a chain to wear round my neck, with a small icon and cross attached to it, and blessed and kissed me three times in the traditional manner of Russian mothers wishing 'God speed' to their departing soldier sons. Late in the afternoon we went to the Aleksandrovski Station in Moscow and assembled on the military platform. With my arms full of flowers, and in a state of exhilaration, I boarded the train to the good wishes of my friends.

We reached Grodzisko, in East Galicia, after a train journey of five days. The town had been captured from the Austrians early in the autumn of the previous year. It was an exciting moment when we left the train. Opposite, above, you see our equipment being unloaded by our orderlies and auxiliaries. I think we all felt that our arrival on captured Austrian territory was the first step in a great mission. Within twenty-four hours we had gathered in the town square, with our vans lined up, ready for the orders that would send us to our work at the Front.

Our destination was Gorlitse, a town some way off in the lower ranges of the Carpathians. The next part of our journey was slow and wearisome, with only occasional stops for rest and refreshment: dry biscuits to eat and packing-cases to sit on. Once or twice, as in the photograph on the left, we halted in a deserted garden. Near Krosno, we took shelter in the Folvark Polyasha. The house, opposite, above, was still untouched, although much of the town of Krosno had been destroyed.

We reached Gorlitse on 11th April, a month after leaving Moscow. Though the Front was very near, we heard the guns only spasmodically. The soldiers, however, told us there were bad signs: German troops and heavy artillery had been sent to this sector of the Austrian Front. It surely pointed to an imminent enemy offensive, and the Germans were a much more formidable prospect than the Austrians.

Feeding the frightened and hungry civilians was a daily task. Our mobile kitchens, like large drums on wheels, were sent into Gorlitse each evening and distributed 300 portions of food to the Austrian townspeople, whose days were spent in the cellars. Meanwhile, we set up our hospital in a local house. Our friends in the Second *Letuchka* moved on to another destination.

On 16th April the guns began to roar and a hail of German shells fell on Gorlitse. The wounded came in hundreds; we worked day and night. On the 19th the order was given to retreat. The chaos and confusion were intensified by continuous enemy bombardment. But gradually the disorder grew less, and I was able to photograph the infantry of the 61st Division, to which we were attached, withdrawing from Jaroslav in perfect marching order.

Below, we had been transferred to the 62nd Division. The retreat was at its height, and our regiments were decimated. Our work continued without a break, though the first wild rush was easing. Here, at Molodych, many wounded and footsore men took refuge at our station.

At the beginning of June, our armies, under the constant enemy barrage, were forced to recross the frontier back into Russian territory. After sharing their hardships for several weeks in open-air bivouacs, we found shelter in the huts of friendly peasants, many of them already suffering their own tragedies. The poor woman opposite, above, was worn out: her husband was missing on the Prussian Front, her elder son was dying of consumption.

When possible, full military honours, sometimes with a band, were accorded to the fighting men who died from wounds. The ceremony was simple: a coffin was made and the soldier laid to rest, wrapped in a sheet and strewn with flowers. Our chaplain, opposite, below, recites the beautiful old Slavonic prayers and the men reverently intone the ancient funeral dirge.

The havoc from the shelling was indiscriminate – a scarred church, a shattered private house. The heaviest type of German shell, with its whistling flight and terrible explosive thud, was nicknamed by the soldiers 'chemodán', a heavy box or trunk.

We were always grateful for the forests. After a long journey over dusty, uneven tracks, their cool serenity could not be expressed in words. If we were to stop for several days, our orderlies would set to work building dug-outs or cabins of pine branches. Opposite, above, are a general's temporary headquarters at Chistaya Smuga. These woodland houses were preferable to our tent life – or so we thought until a day's heavy rain reminded us that a roof of pine branches is not very waterproof.

We were detailed to look after the Mariupolski Regiment, which had suffered severe losses. When they went into reserve in a neighbouring forest in the Chistaya Smuga district, I promised the soldiers I would take photographs of their encampment (opposite, below). My camera proved a great popular success, with the men all clamouring to be photographed at once. The officers persuaded me to join them at supper. When I returned, the sisters were urgently packing. We were retreating again.

At Krasnobrod (opposite, above) we saw wire entanglements and trenches dug in sand, with boards to prevent their sides from collapsing. They gave little protection against the shells. Then, leaving the dunes behind, we reached very different country, with large boulders hindering our passage, where (below) there were trenches hewn out of rock. Under shelling the splinters could be murderous.

These Mariupolski officers, relaxing in the security of the forest, were virtually all to be casualties within a few days. They went into the front line as the order came for us to continue the retreat.

Often, as below, our tents would be set up in the open fields. After their wounds were dressed, the men would be fed and given a rest until transport was available to take them to the base.

We encountered these Cossacks (of the 3rd Circassian Corps) during the June retreat. For them war seemed a natural element and they were trained for it from early childhood – it was even said that they could ride and swim before they could walk. In peacetime they had been constantly used by the Imperial Government to suppress uprisings and control recalcitrants. Their lands were their own, allotted to them under military tenure, and their military organisation was distinct from that of the Imperial Army. It was the Cossacks at this time who carried out the orders to force Russian villagers from their homes and to devastate the countryside in the face of the advancing enemy.

At the end of June we were still in full flight. All over Western Russia the homeless were swarming, Poles and Lithuanians as well as Russians. Their orders consisted of two words – 'Go eastwards!' Taking what they could of their livestock and other possessions, uprooted and helpless, they could but obey and trudge on at random. The family below was typical. Even their horse had collapsed under the physical strain. All they could do was to await another order to move on. There was a military fear that civilians might be forced by the enemy to act as spies. And so for many weeks the life of our *Letuchka* was interwoven with that of the refugees. It was an exodus almost too pitiable to contemplate.

We rested one night in a cornfield near Molodyatyche, less than two miles from the front line. The artillerymen opposite had camouflaged their gun with sheaves. The losses of the Infantry Corps to which our 62nd Division was now attached had been terrible: of 25,000 infantrymen only 2,000 were left. A shortage of ammunition added disastrously to their troubles, and when large quantities of foreign cartridges were finally delivered to the Front, they were found not to fit the Russian rifles.

One of the greatest trials of a Red Cross unit at the front was the complete lack of regular sleep. So (opposite, below) it was a real delight to find a tent provided for us in an orchard, where we could snatch some rest. We depended, too, on the powers of organisation of our housekeeping sister, Yuliya Mikhailovna (right), known as 'Mamasha'. She was an indomitable character of tremendous stamina. She ruled us with a rod of iron, but we obeyed her willingly, recognising her qualities.

Our orchard tent was at Treschany, where I also took the photograph below – of a Russian officer's burial. He had died on his way to our dressing station. We bandaged his head, crossed his arms on his breast, and laid him in his discoloured uniform in an open field. A priest intones the prayers for the dead, and several of our orderlies stand by in homage. No coffin is available; but his name and regiment have been carved on a wooden cross.

On 6th July we arrived in Zanizhe, passing through Teryatin, where I photographed these Russian guns in action. Below is one of our dressing stations, with one tent for the surgical equipment and one for the fatally wounded; and above, opposite, I am working in a makeshift dispensary. In the intervals between tending the wounded we would cut up lint, sterilise bandages, weigh out powders, wrap ingredients in paper, measure and mix liquids. While trains were running, our Red Cross services on railway premises were vital. When we saw the last packed train of casualties slowly steam away, we would say a prayer of gratitude that our injured men were on their way to safety and that our work was, briefly, completed.

After five days in Zanizhe, in mud a foot deep and a plague of flies and insects, we formed up (opposite, above) for our marching orders. Our destination turned out to be Belopolye, where we found that our transport was quite inadequate for the number of wounded. The 62nd Division had stood firm against two enemy attacks during the night, but they had paid severely for their success. The wounded began to come in at dawn and we laid them on straw on the floor of a store-house. A motor-ambulance column providentially came to our aid, with twelve ambulance cars and three lorries. With motor vehicles a rarity, two armoured cars at Belopolye aroused intense interest. The larger one, opposite, below, had its name, 'Mikhailovets', painted on each side, and the captain in charge of it could often be seen carrying his mascot, a small black kitten, in the hollow of his hand.

In Belopolye we spent six hot days in July tending the men of our Division. The group of machine-gunners below were being sent for a short spell in reserve and posed for me with mascots and accordion. Others were less fortunate. The young soldier above was hit by a stray bullet near our station. Sister Anna and one of the doctors soon had him bandaged and resting comfortably. And another unexpected casualty (opposite, below) was Vaska, the 62nd Division's mascot. He had his right hoof slightly crushed by a vehicle. Two orderlies held him down while a surgeon dressed his wound. After bleating frantically throughout his ordeal, he sped away on three legs.

As our soldiers were forced to retreat, they destroyed anything that might afford produce or shelter for the invaders. Sometimes enemy shelling did their work for them: opposite, above, are the remains of a village in the Volhynskaya government.

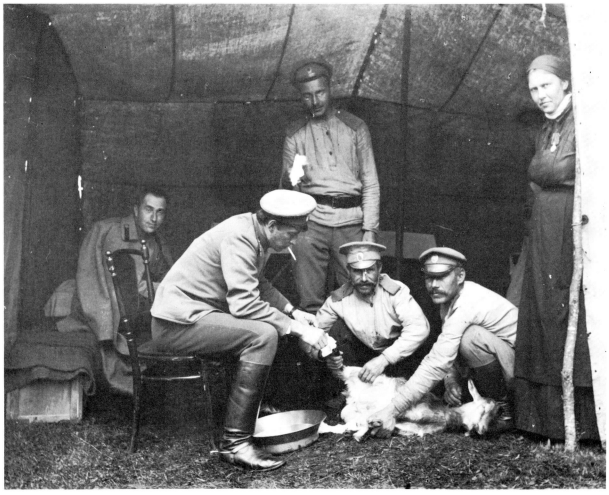

47

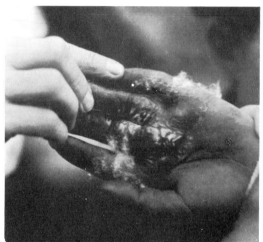

And so the retreat continued. We rested where we could; near Folvark Volka, below, it was under a haystack. There were new horrors: at Zdroya, in August, we had our first experience of the barbaric dum-dum bullets, which burst on impact.

On 17th August we reached the stronghold of Grodno. We saw the well-prepared defences, like the row of dugouts above; we visited the 'invulnerable' forts; then we heard that Grodno was not to be defended but destroyed. We pushed on towards Minsk, sometimes forced to stop – as at Folvark Belinschchizin, opposite, below – by the sheer congestion on the highway. The Cossacks, opposite, from the famous Orenburg Regiment, simulated a firing squad for my camera when we quartered near them at Chertoviche in September.

More than once we were without bread on our road to Minsk. The enormous stores of the Zemstvo depot, even when added to the military ones, could not meet the ever-increasing needs of the retreating masses. Occasionally an open-air regimental bakery would come to our rescue, like the one in these pictures.

By the end of September the pressures upon us receded. The soldiers opposite, at Chertoviche, reflected the new mood of relaxation, though the lonely, unconsecrated graves on the hillside reminded us always of the past weeks' toll. I was given a month's leave, which I spent with the Ousovs in Moscow.

As Christmas drew near, preparations were made for entertaining the refugee children in the forest. In the old dug-out above we hung ornaments and decorated a Christmas tree. The children's faces, already marked with suffering, slowly softened and then shone with excitement.

The festivities continued well into the New Year. We organised musical evenings for the soldiers, and provided high tea for the transport drivers, orderlies and hospital workers. In return, we were hospitably entertained by the Divisional Staff (below) at their headquarters.

By mid-December we had dug ourselves in against the frost and blizzards. All military operations were at a standstill. The soldiers built a small wooden church, perfect in every detail, from the bell to the sacred icon on the altar. Our regimental chaplain officiated and the church was always packed. The military were joined by peasants and refugees and when the congregation overflowed, Mass was said in front of this enormous cross of solid ice, with the altar of ice at its side.

# ADVANCE
## 1916

At Chertoviche (where I took the photograph of some of the 62nd Divisional Staff with their mascot) there was plenty of work to be done for the villagers and refugees, but time for relaxation too – for skiing, skating and tobogganing. A favourite pastime was the revolving wheel, with a small sledge attached to it at the end of a pole. If the wheel were checked, one could be shot from the sledge into the air.

We left Chertoviche on 12th January, in the small hours of the morning. We travelled by train and arrived at Volochisk early on the 17th. Much of the country was still under snow, but spring was not far off and energetic military preparations were afoot on all sides. More than once we saw companies of very raw recruits (like those above) marching past our station. We exchanged greetings and hid the apprehension we felt for them.

Ten days later we were in Chortkov. There were plenty of signs of activity, but the weeks passed without the constantly rumoured 'offensive' becoming a reality. Being the only sister with a camera, I received many commissions in unexpected places. In the rush of daily work, many of the exposed plates were abandoned before they could even be developed. Below, you see me busy with one camera while I am observed by another, and opposite are two more scenes from our stay at Chortkov: above, artillery on the move, and, below, a sledge leaving for a distant dressing station. The gun is drawn by a team of six horses, three pairs in tandem. Some of the gunners rode, while others marched alongside.

We had numerous civilian patients daily at our dispensary. The children suffered pitifully from outbreaks of typhoid, spotted fever and smallpox. Cleanliness was a fearful problem, with the houses overcrowded with lodgers, and even though we set up isolation hospitals, it was virtually impossible to contain the infectious diseases.

The forests bordering the Russian lines afforded both concealment and protection for the troops. The artillery park in the picture above was near Chortkov, and below, near Chertoviche, are some characteristic shacks and dugouts, designed to shelter their occupants from the icy winds. That winter of 1915–16, for all its discomforts, its blizzards and snowdrifts, had come as a friend. After the calamities of the preceding months, we had steadied ourselves. Now there was even better news for our generals. The Germans had transferred much of their strength from our Front back to the Western Front.

When we passed this ancient monastery, of which only a few gaunt corner-pillars remained standing, the trees surrounding its ruined walls were sparkling in the frost as though decked with crystals. Desolation gives a poignancy to beauty; these moments were strangely affecting.

A moving sight, too, was the open-air Mass. The Russian soldiers were naturally religious and there was a feeling of powerful unity as, row upon row, they repeated together the familiar prayers for Tsar, Mother Country, and for the homes and families to which some would never return.

General Vladimir Dragomiroff, himself a general's son, was wounded in Volhynia in the spring of 1916. A more permanent casualty was the railway bridge above, destroyed by the retreating Austrians near Chortkov.

Opposite, above, are soldiers in winter attire and, below, wearing the gas masks which were issued to our unit in early 1916. They gave rise to a good many jokes: the men begged to be photographed in them.

By May the Austrians were retreating rapidly. We were on the move again, this time in an open motor-car (opposite, above), though sometimes in the much more comfortable troop train. Near Rzhepintse, on 27th May, we came upon the Austrian front line trenches, carefully and methodically made, but now battered by our guns. Other trenches (above), quite nearby, had inexplicably escaped the shells and were still intact after being hastily evacuated. What a contrast they were to the ill-prepared ditches to which our soldiers had so often been committed.

Barbed wire entanglements, like those opposite, above, had been intricately constructed to protect the Austrian trenches, sometimes in several rows. It was the duty of the artillery to batter these defences in advance of our troops: I photographed the gunners above during the June fighting.

At the end of May we were billeted with a widow on a farm near Buchach. In the blossoming orchard (opposite, below), among the farmyard animals and birds, we played with the children, refreshed by the beauty of spring and a sense of the newness of life around us. But devastation was never far away. The approaches to Buchach, below, told their own story. The damaged buildings on the high banks of the River Stripa included both the hospital and the sanatorium.

Our members were always inventing pastimes for off-duty hours. Here, near a wooden Austrian church, a target has been set up, to be dislodged by a stick thrown from a given distance. Pastimes such as these were a welcome relaxation, soothing over-stretched nerves. We were paying a price for our continued advance: our tents were packed with wounded, many of them dying. Below, bodies of Russian soldiers lie ready for interment, wrapped in sheets and strewn with flowers.

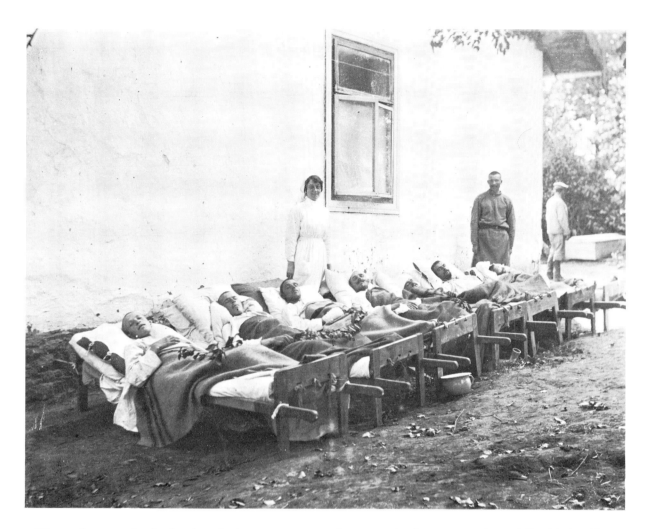

These photographs, both taken during our stay at Buchach in June, show the different faces of routine. Below, at one of our bivouacs, a cook prepares a meal, while his assistant peels potatoes. In the foreground, the inevitable accordion lying between them, two barbers are cutting soldiers' hair. Above, we stay in attendance on the dying when we can, trusting they will find comfort in our presence. A coffin, one of a small stock kept in readiness by our carpenters, stands ominously round the corner.

Often we would watch pityingly from our station in Buchach as a sad little procession of Austrian prisoners filed past. There were Germans, too; in greatcoat and *pickelhaube* (left) one trudges along under mounted escort. The Austrians below were brought to our dressing tent for bandaging.

Near Barish, I was with our forward Red Cross station. In the evening the dead were placed side by side in pit-like graves (opposite, above), swarming with flies. Salvage teams would rescue useful equipment from the battlefield and stack it (opposite, below) in readiness for the men who followed.

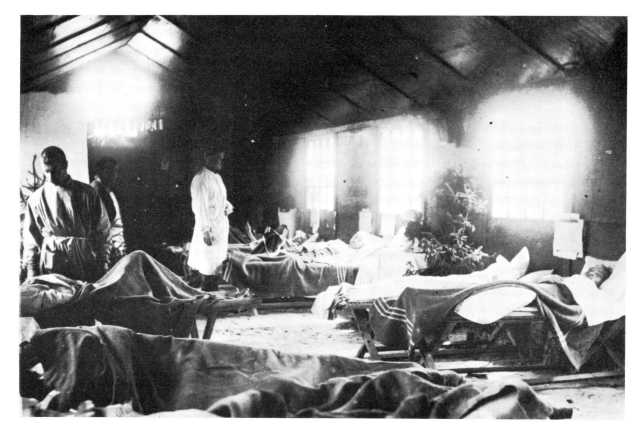

The devastation left by warfare was terrible to see and the loss of life appalling. At Barish a shed, above, provided an excellent hospital ward for the seriously wounded, but our orderlies were faced with the daily task of carrying out burial rites. Our chaplain was usually at hand to officiate; if not, Smirnov, our head orderly, would conduct the emergency funerals (below). His humble integrity and strong faith seemed to add a sanctity to the services, the chant of a choir replaced by the whispering of the trees as he quietly intoned his impromptu prayers.

Mamasha was in her element at these tents, set up near Monasterzhiska to feed soldiers on their way to the base. She was a born supervisor, with a quick eye for the smallest detail, a quick ear for the whispered need, and a quick tongue to reject an unjustified complaint.

Below, on a July day, Sister Vera and I are setting out on a jolting drive to a distant First Aid Post. Our light ambulance vans, frail though they appeared, withstood rough roads and mountain tracks better than heavier vehicles; and their hoods gave protection against the weather.

Everywhere, on the road to Monasterzhiska, were macabre glimpses of the aftermath of battle. Some of the dead (above) lay where they had fallen in that landscape of horror and suffering; others had been laid together in an open-air mortuary, surrounded by forest trees.

Opposite, above the ruins of yet another village home, you see the entrance to an Austrian cemetery. The inscription reads: 'Here rest the heroes fallen for their Fatherland.' Many were Russians; we saw, too, the grave of a Jewish soldier, the Star of David carved above it.

At the beginning of August the advance was checked, with Germans replacing the retreating Austrians. We moved up to Khutanova, passing through these two Galician villages. One was no more than a skeleton; down the central street of the other, Russian sappers had cut a long, zig-zagging line of trenches. One of the village boys pointed cheerfully at the trenches, as if they had been built especially to play in.

The 'home-made' anti-aircraft gun, opposite, above, had been installed in an open field and put into action by its inventors. By revolving the tilted cartwheel, the gunner could fire in any direction.

The monument to our dead, opposite, below, was erected near Khutanova. It was designed by some of the men in our Division.

With the successes of the past weeks behind us, we were confident that our General Brusilov would clear the enemy out of Galicia. Throughout the night of 3rd August, we heard our guns roaring; one of the artillery entrenchments, below, was within walking distance of our camp. Though the guns themselves were somewhat outmoded, our gunners were well trained and inured to hardship. But this time the barrage seemed to be in vain. The enemy's lines remained unbroken.

We stayed at Khutanova for a whole fortnight, in brilliant sunny weather. We made the most of this lull in our work, and one of us would prepare afternoon tea outside the hut (below) where we lodged. Our flower-vase was a spent shell-case, converted to more decorous use.

The bodies of those who succumbed to their wounds were laid aside till evening, and dusk had often fallen before the orderlies returned from their melancholy task (above) of interring the dead.

The army contained many boy soldiers, some of them the mascots of their regiments. Unlike the Carpathian boys in the photograph opposite, above, playing in a deserted Austrian dugout, these boy soldiers found all too soon that a man's part in the trenches was no sort of a game. We could only wonder what their mothers must be feeling.

One day at Khutanova (opposite) I was asked to photograph an Orthodox priest in his coffin. On a visit to the Front he had died from a head wound. The funeral, with full military honours, was attended by several other priests, and a large company of onlookers. It was a nerve-racking experience, but his relatives in Moscow were very grateful.

At the end of August I became severely ill with paratyphoid. As soon as the crisis passed, I was sent for a month to convalesce in the Crimea and in that beautiful setting found the mental and bodily rest I so much needed. It was a joy to be able to sit and read for hours beside the waters of the Black Sea (above). The nurse's veil may look demure but it conceals an embarrassing secret—my head had been shaved. During my illness my hair had got into a desperate condition and the doctors decided on this radical solution. Though I knew it was only a matter of time before the new hair grew in strongly again, I confess that for some while I hardly dared look in a mirror.

I went to Moscow in November and encountered there a general feeling of despondency. On a personal level I was saddened by the illness of Dr. Ousov. He had suffered a severe heart attack, and it was followed by another while I was staying with the family. He was to live only until the beginning of January, the report of his death coming close upon the news from home that my father too had died. I was by this time back with my beloved unit at Trebukhovtsy, where the suspension of military operations on the Southern Front left us little of importance to do. It was a time for grief.

# INTO REVOLUTION
## 1917-1918

The end of 1916, with the murder of Rasputin, had brought a period of speculation. Then, in March, we were stunned by the news of the Tsar's abdication. As firm royalists we felt deeply for him and his family. But the provisional regime, in patriotic hands, not only preserved law and order, but stimulated the public spirit. At the Front manifestoes began to be widely distributed, proclaiming the soldiery's new Freedom. The Germans, on the other hand, saw it as an opportunity to distribute their own propaganda, hoping to spread unrest in the Russian trenches with promises of peace.

The photograph below was taken in June near Bozikov, in the Carpathians. We devised these horse-drawn stretchers because the narrow tracks were often blocked by ambulance vans and carts. By following the mountain paths that branched off the main tracks, we could get the wounded down more quickly to somewhat greater comfort. On one side, at Bozikov, were lofty mountain peaks, and on the other several lovely green valleys, their little villages now, sadly, ruined and deserted. We raised our tents among fine old mountain trees for a few hours of unbroken rest.

A company of reinforcements arrived near our station during the summer. To our great surprise they were not Russians at all, but Khirgiz from Western Turkestan, near the Aral Sea. Mongol in origin, they were nomads, well seasoned to open-air hardship. But it seemed incredible that these—to us—strange-looking Asiatics should be recruited into the Imperial Russian Army.

The days spent in the cool forest near Bozikov were a blessing to us all. Above is a view of part of our encampment, and below the men of our unit gather in a carefully posed group. Only the dog in the foreground seems to have escaped the air of general concentration! Temporarily relieved from the usual pressures, the men were cheerful, singing their traditional songs around the camp fire.

While at Podgaytsy, in May 1917, we had word that Kerensky himself was coming to address the troops. His reforms, designed to create a closer relationship between the men and their officers, were having the reverse effect. A huge crowd turned out to hear him; to our great good fortune some regimental doctors helped us through to the front row. Kerensky was an extraordinarily hypnotic speaker. His theme was 'Freedom': the soldiers must fight for Free Mother Russia, they must drive the enemy off Russian soil. 'We will!' they shouted with boundless enthusiasm. When he left, they carried him on their shoulders to his car.

Despite disheartening reports from Petrograd, military operations were stepped up. In Loschina, at the beginning of June, we were invited to see some aerostats, captive balloons, that were grounded in the area. We watched one of them, opposite, being launched. When the tethering ropes were released, there was a tense minute or two of complete silence. Then, as the enormous, unwieldy balloon rose slowly into the air, the spectators cheered excitedly. Soon it was high in the air, with the observer in his wicker cage and a large ballast-bag hanging over its side.

The balloons were moored to the ground, at the mercy of marauding enemy aeroplanes, and the observer had a parachute in case of attack. Only two days after this launching, two of the four balloons were hit by enemy incendiary bullets, and the men in them, failing to jump in time, died in the flames.

A mystery I never solved was whether the flag in the photograph below had any particular significance. On one of our journeys, through a small Galician town, I saw this White Ensign flying from the upper

storey of a terraced house. It gave me a nostalgic shock of recognition. No one could tell me anything about it, not even the name of the town.

For a few stormy days in early July, we took refuge in a cow-barn (above). The news from our Front grew worse daily. There were many desertions, and the enemy had taken possession of the empty trenches. By the time we reached Grabuvka, where the photograph below was taken of our *Letuchka*, our situation was so uncertain that we did not even unpack. Rumours were circulating about insubordination at the Front. When, in late July, we were ordered into Roumania, we were delighted. The Roumanians were our allies, already fighting successfully alongside Russian troops. Fears for the disbandment of our unit receded: there would be work to do.

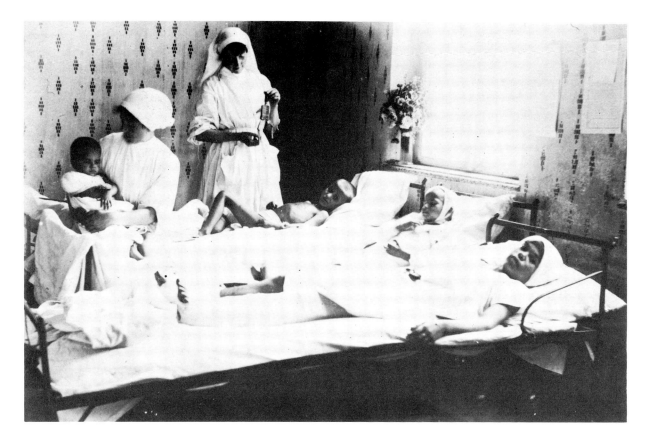

We found that relations between the Russian and Roumanian soldiers were far from harmonious, and the peasantry viewed us with suspicion. Stores had been raided and property looted.

Three of our patients in Seret were from the Bachkarova Women's Death Battalion. This had been recruited in Russia by the Siberian woman soldier, Yasha Bachkarova. Very few of her 2,000 volunteers came up to her standards; the battalion dwindled to 250, and many of those let her down when called into the attack.

There were also wounded children in the hospital. One of them, Gheorghi (below), a two-year-old, had lost his right arm, blasted off by shrapnel.

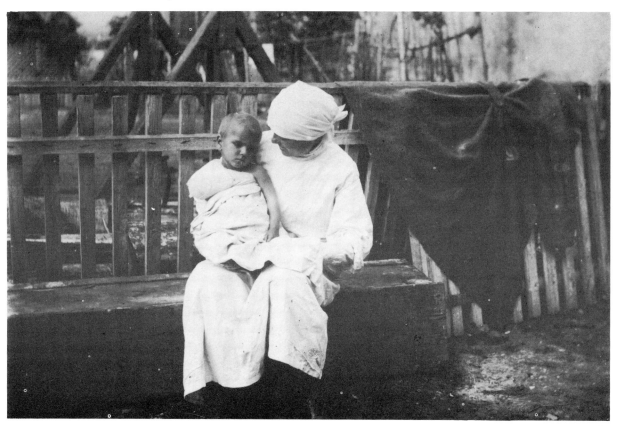

Sometimes we encamped in the open air. Above, at Loupeni, where we are grouped beside the River Prut, we spent three restful days, sleeping at night on the hillside. Below, our camp beds are lined up on the banks of the River Suchava, near Izkani, with a night-time chorus of frogs to keep us company.

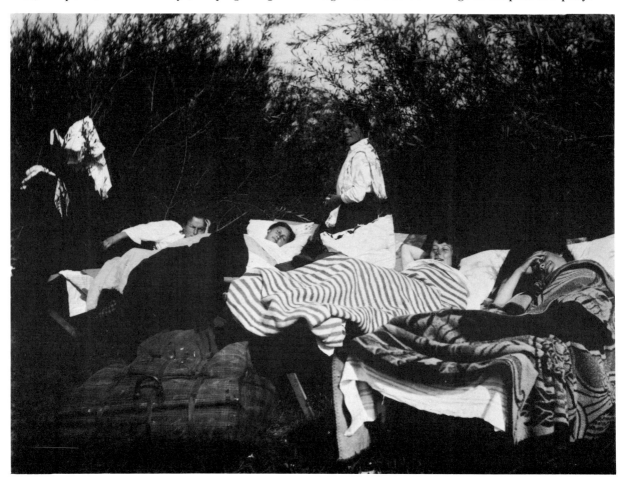

In spring, the sheep would be collected in the villages and driven up the trackless slopes of the lower Carpathians, where there were rich pastures. These three generations of shepherds, above, took their pastoral migration as a matter of course, and spent the summer in a rough brushwood wigwam.

They would return when the autumn frosts began.

In the village of Kloster Gumora, below, I took several photographs of the woman who put us up so kindly. Having grouped her family, she disappeared into the hut to put on her husband's boots, one of the household's proudest possessions.

In Roumania, harvesting (opposite, above) was a pleasant social occasion. The plains produced fine crops of wheat and maize, the peasants' staple diet. As the war dragged on, food grew scarce, and many peasants refused to sell their produce. However, one family, opposite, below, let us share their splendid melons, marrows and pumpkins.

We had not expected subversive elements on the Roumanian Front. Above, paid agents are persuading our soldiers that a life of freedom could only be achieved by a refusal to go on fighting.

The Turkish prisoners below were brought to us at the beginning of September. We had to scrape the mud and vermin off them before we could treat them.

And so began the undoing. These soldiers, above, had forsaken the Imperial Army and joined the Red Revolutionary Army, under the banner of Freedom, inscribed here with the Russian words for 'Liberty, Equality, Fraternity'. For them, the aspirations; for those commemorated on the Roumanian hillside below, only the serenity of sacrifice. The Bolsheviks, fearing the authority of religion, persecuted it bitterly from the start. Opposite, above, a church has been desecrated; below, a Bolshevik ransacks a private house, destruction his motive force. Theft and sabotage were rampant: 'What's yours is mine' was the new slogan, rounded off with 'What's mine is my own.'

In November I went on leave to Moscow, where I stayed with my Russian 'family' for nearly three weeks before rejoining my unit in Roumania. There, we heard that civil war had begun in earnest. The unit was disbanded; we were told to make our way to Moscow as best we could.

I took the two photographs opposite in December 1917, as the Russian army straggled away from the Roumanian Front, deserting their allies for home and the dream of freedom.

I stayed two nights in Odessa with a kindly doctor and his doctor wife (she had been with us briefly in Roumania). Red Guards were in control of both the city and the seaport. After a terrible week-long train journey, I found myself once again in Moscow.

In February 1918, the Bolshevik Government signed the Treaty of Brest-Litovsk with Germany. Famine was rife, for production and distribution alike were at a standstill. Sorrowfully leaving my friends, I took a ticket in March on the last goods train running direct to Vladivostok on the Trans-Siberian Railway. Our motley crew of refugees, of many nationalities, jerked across the Urals in wooden trucks, then over the snow-covered steppes. The silence and peace of that vast sleeping world was a tonic after the violence and turmoil of Moscow. In Eastern Siberia, above, all there was to see was an occasional railway station, or group of wooden shanties, the homes of political exiles.

Yasha Bachkarova, right, was among the few Russians who escaped to Vladivostok. She had fought in the trenches at her husband's side, and fought on after his death. Wounded twice and decorated for valour three times, she was raised by Kerensky to the rank of officer.

95

After a journey of twenty-seven days, our 'coal-scuttle', as we nicknamed our fourth-class carriage, at last reached Vladivostok. On the calm surface of the great harbour lay four warships. From the terminus we saw, to our overwhelming joy and surprise, that one of the cruisers was flying a British flag. It was impossible to express our feelings after three and a half years of war on alien soil: it was like a familiar voice saying 'Welcome home'.

From the hills above Vladivostok the view (below) was superb. Besides H.M.S. *Suffolk*, there were two Japanese ships and an American cruiser: for us, and for all the foreigners in the town, they represented safety. Far away, to the right, was the Sea of Japan, and, beyond, the immense expanse of the Pacific. In my daydreams I was already on the welcoming shores of America, from where I was to sail on for England and for home